A Discovery Biography

Elizabeth Blackwell

—◆—

Pioneer Woman Doctor

by Jean Lee Latham
illustrated by Ethel Gold

CHELSEA JUNIORS
A division of Chelsea House Publishers
New York ◆ Philadelphia

To George W. Rosner of the University of Miami for
helpfulness above and beyond the call of duty

The Discovery Books have been prepared under the
educational supervision of Mary C. Austin, Ed.D.,
Reading Specialist and Professor of Education, Case
Western Reserve University.

Cover illustration: Janet Hamlin

First Chelsea House edition 1991

3 5 7 9 8 6 4 2

ISBN 0-7910-1406-1

Contents

Chapter *1*

New Worlds

Mary, the maid, came in, looking glum. "A Mr. Anderson to see you, sir."

Father flipped through some papers and looked at a letter. "Anderson? Oh, yes! About the position as tutor."

"Yes, sir. Another one."

"Then show him in." Father stood up, smiled, and winked at the girls.

Elizabeth wriggled, trying to hold back her giggles. Father was more fun than anybody in the whole town of Bristol. Maybe in all of England!

A young man came in. "Mr. Blackwell, I'm Robert Anderson." He looked around the big, handsome room with two pianos, one on each side of the fireplace.

Father shook hands. "These are my oldest daughters, Mr. Anderson. Anna is thirteen, Marian is eleven, and Elizabeth is eight."

Mr. Anderson nodded at the girls.

"Sit down, Mr. Anderson. I see you have a good education. Latin, German, mathematics—"

"Yes, sir. And philosophy, literature, and history. From Cambridge, sir."

"All important. Also, I want my daughters to have—"

"Your daughters? But where are your sons?"

Father smiled. "They are a little young. Sam is six. Henry is four."

Mr. Anderson jumped up. "You—you mean you want a tutor for your girls?"

"And why not? My girls are thinking creatures. I want them to have the same education my sons will have."

"But—but—sir!"

"Yes, Mr. Anderson?"

"I—I—good-bye!"

Mary was at the door. "Your hat, sir."

Elizabeth counted. "That makes nine who won't teach girls."

Father chuckled. "You're a thinking creature even at the age of eight. I'll see you girls at tea." He went out.

Marian said, "It's too bad poor old Mr. Winshore got sick."

Anna shrugged and laughed. "But it's fun to hear father talk to all these others. I wonder how many more there will be?"

Fifteen shocked young men walked in and walked out before Miss Eliza Major came. She had a fine education and was not a bit shocked about teaching girls.

When Elizabeth was ten father was as jolly as ever. But sometimes, when he did not know that anybody was watching, he looked worried.

Suddenly one day Mr. Blackwell said he wanted the family to go to their home in the country.

Mother always said, "Yes, Samuel," to anything father said. But now she said, "Samuel, I will not go one step until you tell us what's wrong."

"Why, Hannah!"

Very gently she repeated, "Not one step."

At last he explained. Times were

hard, and money was scarce. Men were losing their jobs. They were angry. He was afraid there might be trouble.

"Samuel! Then you must come with us!"

"Nonsense. I'm in no danger."

Father owned the biggest sugar refinery in Bristol, where men turned molasses into sugar. He paid his men well, and he took care of them when they were sick.

"My men know I've stood up for them," he went on. "They will not wreck our plant."

Mother, Miss Major, the servants, and the children went to the country.

One evening father came. He looked very tired and he spoke quietly. His plant had been burned.

"Samuel! What will we do now?"

He straightened. There was a light in his eyes. "We'll go to America and start over again in a new world!"

Mother looked ready to cry. Marian did cry. But Elizabeth hugged herself. All her life she had loved to look at the ships in the harbor. Now she would sail on a ship, on a long, long voyage!

In August of 1832 they sailed from Liverpool. Elizabeth found a place where she could stay on deck, out of the way, and watch the white sails spread.

That was her last happy time. Before morning she was more sick than she had ever been in her whole life.

Chapter 2

Another New World

"Don't worry, Elizabeth," Miss Major said. "You'll feel fine soon."

But Elizabeth did not "feel fine soon." Week after week, for almost eight weeks, she was miserable.

At last they reached America and settled in New York City. Now Elizabeth could look at the ships in the harbor. She loved to look at them—from the shore.

After a time they moved to a big house in New Jersey.

In England Uncle Charles had loved Miss Major. Now he came to America and married her. The children's Miss Major was now Aunt Eliza!

Uncle Charles and Aunt Eliza started a private school in New York. The younger girls went there. The boys went to a school for boys.

Happy days ended in 1837. Hard times came to America. Father admitted he was worried.

Father heard that times were not so hard farther west, on the Ohio River. Early in 1838 he took a trip to see for himself.

He came back, looking very tired, but with that special light in his eyes again. "We're moving to Cincinnati, Ohio! It's a beautiful little town!"

They packed only books, one piano, and a few special pieces of furniture.

A friend would sell their house, the furniture, and the business.

Anna and Marian were teaching, so Elizabeth, now seventeen, was the oldest of the children to go to Cincinnati. It was a long, hard trip, by stagecoach, canal boat, and then a riverboat on the Ohio River.

At last they reached Cincinnati.

Father found a house and bought furniture on credit. When the friend back East sold everything and sent father the money, he would pay his bills.

But shocking news came from the East. The "friend" who had sold everything disappeared with the money.

"I can borrow more money," father said. "Men here believe in me."

But father died suddenly. He left his family with nothing but debts, doctor bills, and just $25 in cash.

Chapter *3*

The Challenge

Elizabeth was stunned with grief. But there was no time to sit and weep. She had to help mother.

Anna and Marian came home. The three girls opened a school. Sam, who was fifteen, marched in one day and said he had a job at the courthouse. Soon Henry got a job too.

Sam and Henry seemed to have a gift for making money. After a few years they said they could take care of the family.

The girls closed their school. Anna began writing for newspapers. Marian was content to stay home. But Elizabeth paced the floor and wondered what to do with her life.

One day she visited a friend of her mother. The woman was dying. She said, "Elizabeth, why don't you become a doctor? The first woman doctor in America! You have health and brains." She smiled faintly. "And I suspect that when you were little they said you were stubborn."

"Yes, very stubborn."

"If I could have had a woman doctor, she would have understood me better."

For days Elizabeth thought about it. She was already 24. How long would it take to become a doctor? Where could she go to study?

She talked to their doctor. He was shocked. Impossible! No medical school would admit a woman! She talked to her friends. Most of them were horrified.

But one told her about the Reverend John Dickson in Asheville, North Carolina. He needed a teacher in his private school. Before he became a minister, he had been a doctor. He had a fine medical library.

Elizabeth told her family about it. "I feel it's a signpost pointing to the way I should go," she said.

She wrote to John Dickson. Before his answer came, she was already planning what she would pack.

At last his answer did come. He would be delighted to have her teach in his school. She could live in his home, read his medical books, and save her salary for going to medical college.

Her brothers, Sam and young Howard, offered to drive her to Asheville.

So Elizabeth set out to do the impossible. As her mother's friend had said, Elizabeth had health, brains, and stubbornness. Would her stubbornness be the most important?

Soon she was working long hours. By day she taught reading and music. At night she read medical books. How much there was to learn! Just the names of things would take forever! There were about 200 bones and 400 muscles, and that was just the beginning.

In December John Dickson had bad news—and good. He was closing his school. But his brother, Dr. Samuel H. Dickson, a fine doctor in Charleston, South Carolina, had offered to help Elizabeth. She could live in his home, teach in a fine girls' school there, and study in his medical library.

At first Dr. Dickson said, "I'll help you, but I don't promise anything." After a few months he said, "You're amazing! I'll write to my friends in the medical schools in Philadelphia."

Answers from Philadelphia all said the same thing. A woman in a medical college? Never! But two doctors did offer to help her with private study.

"Go there!" Dr. Dickson said. "You may amaze those doctors so much they will admit you to a college."

"Thank you, Dr. Dickson!"

"The best way to go will be by ship up the coast," the doctor said.

Another ship! Maybe she would not get sick this time. But she did.

Chapter *4*

A Strange Welcome

Dr. Elder and his wife welcomed Elizabeth. She boarded with them and read the doctor's medical books.

"You have learned a great deal," Dr. Elder said. "I'll help you all I can with your studies. And I'll do everything I can to help you find a medical school that will admit you."

A Dr. Allen offered to teach her in his school of anatomy. She could come in the evening, when no men students would be there. Her first night in his laboratory, she almost fainted. She had to learn to dissect—to cut into a part of a dead body.

With Dr. Elder's help she wrote to
every big medical school in America.
They all said no! She got catalogs
from all the smaller colleges. With Dr.
Elder's help, Elizabeth wrote to twelve
of them. One by one they said no!

October came. There was no time
to lose. Medical schools were opening.
Elizabeth was 26. For almost three
years she had worked night and day.

Finally a letter came from Geneva
Medical College in western New York
State. The faculty had let the student
body vote on whether or not they
should admit a woman. The students
had voted yes! They would welcome
Miss Elizabeth Blackwell!

She would be starting late, but at
last she could begin! She smiled to
herself all the way to Geneva.

Elizabeth got a room in a hotel

when she arrived, then went out to find a boardinghouse.

Three landladies said, "No rooms!"

"But you have a sign out!" Elizabeth said to the third one.

"Not for the kind of woman who'd be a doctor!"

She stayed in the hotel overnight. The next day she started to hunt again for a boardinghouse.

At last a Miss Waller took her in. "I don't know how you'll get along in that college," she said. "The boys are so rowdy that some people want to close the school."

"I'm sure I'll get along," Elizabeth said. "I have four younger brothers."

She moved into her room. Then she went to the college. The boys stared at her and whispered to each other. What was wrong?

The faculty seemed stiff and uneasy. The professor of anatomy was away. His assistant would not let Elizabeth in the class. She had never felt so unwelcome in her life.

It was a long time before she learned the truth. The faculty had not wanted to admit her. They thought they could dodge the problem by letting the students vote on it. So the faculty had said the vote must be unanimous, without a single no. Those boys never agreed about anything!

But the boys had thought it was a joke. Maybe some other school was playing a trick on them. So they voted to admit her. The faculty had to go along with that vote.

Then Dr. Webster, the roly-poly, jolly little professor of anatomy, arrived. He greeted her with smiles. After that, the mood of the students changed.

After two days Dr. Webster said, "My dear Miss Blackwell, you are a lion tamer! Our boys have been so rowdy that you could hardly hear yourself talk. Now they are behaving like perfect gentlemen."

But the people in the boardinghouse still did not speak to her. The women of the town stared and whispered. Elizabeth heard the gossip. She was "either mad or bad." Only a crazy woman, or a wicked one, would try to be a doctor!

Elizabeth had never been so alone in her life. She went to school, sat in classes, and took notes. She walked out, keeping her eyes straight ahead. The boys were friendly enough in class, but she never saw them outside the college.

Chapter *5*

The Accident

Christmas Day Elizabeth was alone in her room. She read the Christmas letter from home. Every year all the family wrote something for it.

She spent New Year's Eve alone. She practiced making a speech, knowing that someday she might have to talk to groups of people about medicine. She practiced for an hour, then shook her head. Her medical studies were hard, but learning to make a speech was much harder!

The school "year" at Geneva was only four months, from October through January. The Elders invited Elizabeth to come back to Philadelphia for the summer. Dr. Elder could not find a hospital that would admit her, but he thought she could get a job in the Blockley Almshouse. It was a huge place that cared both for the poor and the sick.

Elizabeth got a job at Blockley for the summer. The young doctors who worked there glared at her. They were supposed to fill in a card on each patient's bed, telling about the patient. When Elizabeth started to work in one part of the hospital, the young doctors stopped filling out cards on those beds.

Elizabeth only smiled. It just meant that she would have to figure out what was wrong with a patient, without the doctors' help. It was good practice!

But in October she was glad to leave Blockley and go back to Geneva.

The women of Geneva still stared and whispered. But she was welcomed at the college. The faculty respected her as one of their best students. The boys welcomed her as their "big sister." It seemed like home!

In January all the senior students had to take examinations to see if they would get their M.D. degrees. After Elizabeth had taken her examination, the teachers said, "Congratulations! You have made the top marks."

Young Howard, now almost 20, came to see his sister get her degree. Graduation exercises were to be held in the Presbyterian Church. The faculty thought quite a few women would want to come, so they made a rule that the women would be seated first.

More women than they had planned for swarmed in, both from the town and from the countryside. The men had to wait until after the graduates marched in. Then they stood in the aisles.

The graduates were called up, four at a time. The president spoke to them and gave them their diplomas. Then Elizabeth was called up alone. The president stood and removed his hat as he gave her the first medical diploma awarded to a woman in America.

She was now Dr. Elizabeth Blackwell. But she knew there was one more giant step to take before she could open her office and begin to help people. She must have a chance to be an intern, a doctor in training, in some hospital.

Her teachers at Geneva had talked about where she should go to intern. What about Paris? The doctors there were world famous. Many American doctors had trained in Paris hospitals. They might not accept a woman doctor, but she could disguise herself as a man and get in that way.

"I'll not go in disguise!" Elizabeth said. "I'll make my way as a woman!"

Her brothers offered her money to go on with her studies. Her Cousin Kenyon wrote from Boston. He was sailing for England soon. Would she like to go with him?

Elizabeth sighed. She would have to make another ocean voyage. She'd make two voyages—first to England and then to France. She had made up her mind. Somehow she would find a way to intern in a hospital in Paris!

Maybe these voyages would not be so bad? They were worse! But by the time she got to Paris, she was over her seasickness and full of hope.

One after another the hospitals said no. There was only one hospital she could enter. La Maternité was the biggest maternity hospital in the world. Young peasant girls from all over France were trained there as midwives. Then they went back to little villages that had no doctors, to help women in childbirth.

Elizabeth could enter La Maternité, but not as a doctor. She would work along with the peasant girls.

Her sister Anna arrived in Paris to write foreign news for American papers. She learned about La Maternité. She argued, stormed, and finally wept. "You can't go there! You'll be shut inside those walls like a prisoner. You'll never see a newspaper. You'll be treated like a servant."

"But I'll see more of one part of medicine in three months there than I'd see in ten years anywhere else."

"Oh, how can you be so stubborn?"

Elizabeth smiled. "It's a great help."

On June 30, 1849, she said good-bye to Anna and went into the hospital. Her days began at 5:30 A.M. When she was "on duty" she worked twelve hours. Three or four times a week she was on duty all night.

But how much she was learning! At least once a week, and sometimes more often, a famous surgeon was called in to do a special operation.

She wrote to Cousin Kenyon in England about her plans. First she would finish training at La Maternité.

Then she wanted to become a surgeon. She would need a chance to intern in a good hospital. Maybe he could help her.

"The first woman surgeon!" She was thinking of that as she put medicine in the eyes of a baby. The light was dim, and she leaned closer. Some of the liquid splashed out of the baby's infected eye and into her left eye.

By evening her left eye was itching. Had she caught the disease from the baby's eye?

In the morning both her eyelids were stuck shut. She sent for Monsieur Blot, the head intern. Could she leave La Maternité until her eyes felt better?

"No!" he shouted. "You need help right now. It's the only chance to save your eye."

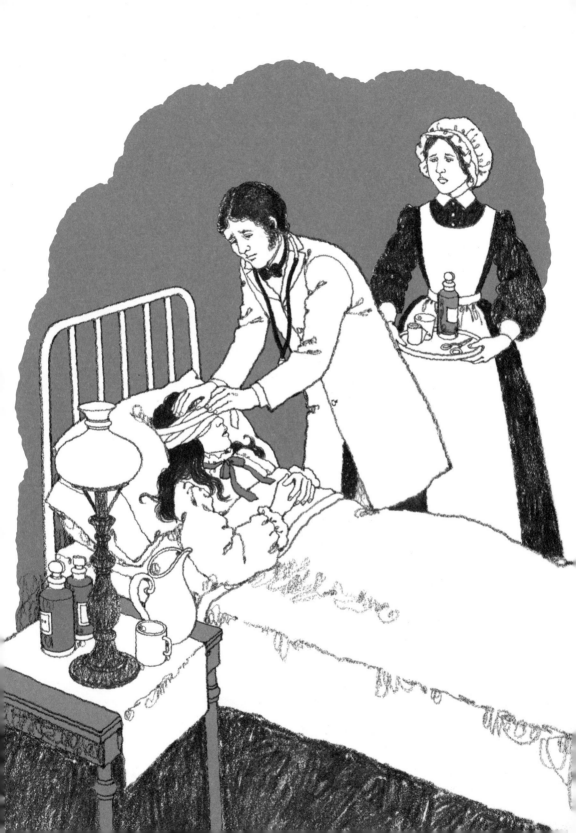

Chapter 6

Elizabeth Makes a Choice

Monsieur Blot ordered that Elizabeth be moved to a quiet place in the infirmary. He came back soon with a nurse. "I have been relieved of other duty to take care of you."

For five days Monsieur Blot and a nurse took care of Elizabeth. Hour after hour, day and night, one or the other was with her.

After three weeks the head of the hospital let Elizabeth go home to Anna's apartment in Paris. Monsieur Blot came there to call on her.

Elizabeth tried to study. It was no use. If she used her right eye, the left eye swelled and ached. At last Monsieur Blot told her the grim truth. She was blind in her left eye.

In May word came from Kenyon. "I have great news, Elizabeth! St. Bartholomew's Hospital in London will admit you to intern there!"

In the same mail there was a letter from James Paget, head of St. Bartholomew's, with a card of admission for Elizabeth. For once Elizabeth wept. Her chance had come, and it was too late. She could never be a surgeon!

Well, she told herself, there were other kinds of doctors. But before she could begin her work at St. Bartholomew's, she must get back her health.

She wrote to Kenyon, telling him of the accident. She wrote to James Paget and thanked him for the chance to intern in St. Bartholomew's. She would be there, she said, as soon as she recovered her usual good health.

She went to a health resort in Germany, to build up her strength. The cold baths and long walks made her feel better. But after a few weeks her left eye hurt as it never had before. She hurried back to Paris. The left eye had to be removed to save the right eye.

By October of 1850 Elizabeth was fitted with a glass eye, and her right eye was getting stronger every day. She had lost almost nine months of time since the accident. But at last she could go to London and to St. Bartholomew's. She had her health again, her brains—and her stubbornness.

Letters from her sister Emily cheered Elizabeth. Emily was teaching now and saving her money. She was going to follow in Elizabeth's footsteps and be the next Dr. Blackwell!

"Maybe," Elizabeth thought, "she will go where I can't go. She will be the first woman surgeon."

Days working in the hospital were long. Evenings in her rooms were lonely. Then three girls came to see her—Barbara Leigh Smith, Barbara's sister, and a friend. They had heard about the first woman doctor. They admired her. They wanted to make something of their lives.

Soon the three girls seemed almost like sisters to Elizabeth, for they had grown up in families that believed "girls are thinking creatures" too.

Elizabeth spent happy evenings in their homes, meeting famous writers, artists, and scientists. All these important people made Elizabeth feel welcome. They promised to do all they could to interest their people in training women doctors. But nothing happened. In England, as it had been in America, the colleges said no.

One day Barbara's cousin came to see Elizabeth. "I'm Florence Nightingale," she said.

From that day on the two spent many hours together. They talked of ways to care for the sick. Sometimes they were together in London, in Elizabeth's little rooms. Sometimes they walked the grounds of the huge Nightingale home.

"Stay in England!" Florence begged. "Let me work with you. If I could work with you, I know I could make something of my life."

But Elizabeth shook her head. America was going to be the first country to let women doctors practice. The pioneering must begin there. Elizabeth knew that she must go back to America when her training at St. Bartholomew's was complete.

Florence went to a nursing school in Germany. She wrote about her life there. It sounded as harsh as Elizabeth's days in La Maternité. But, Florence wrote, she had never been so happy!

The summer of 1851 Elizabeth went back to New York City. She had been gone from America only two years, but sometimes it had seemed like ten.

Elizabeth was glad to be home. She

couldn't wait to begin her new life! She had letters from La Maternité, from St. Bartholomew's, and from several doctors, praising her work.

She went to a dispensary, where poor people could come, talk to a doctor, and get free advice and free medicine. She showed the head doctor her record and asked if she could work there.

He curled his lip in a sneer. "You'd better set up your own dispensary!"

Chapter 7

No Welcome Home

That was a sample of Elizabeth's "welcome home." She could not find rooms for her office. One landlady after another shut the door in her face. A woman doctor? Never!

At last she rented the whole floor of a house, at two times what it should have cost.

She went to a newspaper office. The editor knew Anna. Would he put an announcement in his paper about Dr. Blackwell? He would! So all of New York City knew that Dr. Elizabeth Blackwell, just returned from study in Paris and London, had opened her offices at 44 University Place.

Elizabeth sat in the office and waited. Nothing in all her years of study and work was as hard as those empty days. If it had not been for the money her brothers sent her, she would not have had enough to eat.

Health, brains, training—they did not help. She had nothing left but her stubbornness. She spent her time writing and rewriting lectures over and over again. Then she practiced saying them.

The next spring she rented a basement room in a church and announced that she would give six lectures for two dollars. About three dozen women came. Some were shocked at what she had to say about the health education of girls. They stalked out and did not come back. But one group stayed. They were members of the Society of Friends—the Quakers.

Soon they were coming to her office as patients. Later they gave Elizabeth money to start a dispensary. It was small—just one room in a crowded tenement region, where poor women and children could be treated free by a woman doctor. Elizabeth kept the dispensary open three afternoons a week. At first the poor were as wary of a woman doctor as other people. Then they began to come.

Elizabeth was busy now. But how she missed having another doctor to talk to. If only Emily were through medical college and could be with her.

But Emily had had a hard time getting into a college. Even Geneva would not take her. The State Medical Association of New York had laid down the law: "No more women."

Rush College in Chicago had finally admitted Emily. Her letters were happy. They were the bright spot in Elizabeth's days. She needed some bright spots. Her landlady made all the trouble she could. Elizabeth tried to find other rooms. It was impossible. The only thing to do, she decided, was to buy her own house.

With the help of a friend, she made the first payment. She rented most of the house to a family that took in roomers. She kept the front parlor for an office, and she lived in the attic.

Emily came to spend the summer with her. She was having wonderful luck! The huge Bellevue Hospital was going to let her visit the wards. Of course, she was not an intern yet, but she could learn a lot.

One night she came home with even

more exciting news. The great doctor, James Young Simpson, of Edinburgh, Scotland, had talked to her. If she kept up her fine record at Rush and got her diploma, he would take her as his assistant for special training.

Elizabeth remembered her own early days of study. Medical schools would not admit her, but doctors did help her study outside the colleges. Many doctors had helped her, but nobody so great as James Young Simpson!

"Just as soon as I finish at Rush," Emily said, "my dark days are over!"

But Rush College would not admit Emily for her second year. The State Medical Association of Illinois had laid down the law too: "No more women."

Chapter *8*

Kitty

After a long hunt, Emily entered Western Reserve College in Cleveland, Ohio. In March of 1854 she finished with the highest honors. At that time ten points indicated the highest record. The faculty gave her eleven points. They also wrote a special letter about her, and every man on the faculty signed it.

Elizabeth cheered with her and helped her get ready to go to Edinburgh. She smiled as she kissed Emily good-bye. Then she turned back to her lonely life with no doctor to talk to.

In May a tall, vigorous young woman came to her door. She held out a card with a printed name: Marie Zakrzewska. She smiled and pronounced it: "zak-SHEF-ska." She tried to speak English. Elizabeth answered in German.

Marie beamed and told about herself. She was Polish, but she had trained in Germany. She came from a long line of midwives. She had held a top position in a big hospital, but the man who had appointed her died. The other doctors managed to fire her. She had come to America, for she wanted to be a doctor. To earn her living, she had been doing needlework. For a sixteen-hour day, she was paid 50¢. A Quaker had sent her to Dr. Blackwell.

Elizabeth could have shouted for joy. At last she had someone to talk to and to work with! They made a good bargain. Marie would work with Elizabeth. Elizabeth would teach Marie English and help her prepare to enter Western Reserve College.

When Marie went to Cleveland in the fall, Elizabeth sent her off with a smile. Then Elizabeth shook her head. In medicine, Marie was a genius. But, oh, what she did to the English language!

Again the office seemed empty. How she would miss Marie!

Elizabeth's sister Marian came for a short visit. Marian had an idea. An orphans' home nearby cared for immigrant children. Their parents had died on the journey to America. Many families were adopting one of these little boys or girls.

"A nice, sturdy little girl of ten or twelve would be a big help to you,"

Marian said. "And you'd be good for her. You've always had a way with children."

They went to the home and saw the children. There were more than 400 right then, the matron said. She brought forward one sturdy little girl after another and told about each one. But Elizabeth was looking at a scrawny little child with blinking eyes.

"Tell me about her," she said.

The matron was very surprised. Kitty Barry would never do. "She's only seven, and she's not very strong. Probably rather stupid."

"I want to talk to her."

The matron sighed and went to fetch the child.

"Elizabeth!" Marian gasped. "Why?"

"She needs me more than any of the others do."

The matron came back with Kitty. "Really, Dr. Blackwell—"

"It's no use," Marian said. "She is indeed the most stubborn woman in the world."

Elizabeth knelt by the little girl. "Kitty, would you like to come home for a visit with me?"

Kitty beamed. "Oh, yes, doctor!"

"Not so stupid," Elizabeth thought. "She picked up the word 'doctor' right away."

After a few weeks Elizabeth said, "Kitty, we are going to the home today for something special. Can you guess what?"

Kitty bowed her head. "Yes, doctor."

"I'm going to adopt you. You'll be my little girl forever and ever."

"Oh, doctor! My doctor!"

The matron could not believe the change in Kitty. "She's so bright, so lively! What in the world has happened?" she asked.

"Exercise," Elizabeth said. "The world pays so much attention to education —of a sort—for girls, and no attention at all to building a healthy body. I wish to adopt Kitty." She smiled. "And my sister was right about me. I am stubborn. Very stubborn."

Sometimes, when Kitty was not in school, Elizabeth took her to the dispensary.

One afternoon, as they were coming home, a big dog raced around the corner and knocked Kitty down. He had an old metal pan tied to him, and he was frantic. But the minute Kitty fell, he stopped by her and whimpered.

Kitty sat up and hugged him. "Oh, doctor, he *needs* us!"

Elizabeth understood. She untied the pan, and they took "Lion" home.

Once she heard Kitty talking to him. "We have adopted you, Lion. Do you know what that means? You are our dog. Forever and ever!"

Startling news came from Emily. England was at war with Russia. Heavy fighting was going on in the Crimea (kry-MEE-uh), part of the southern coast of Russia that jutted into the Black Sea. Wounded British soldiers in the Crimea had been dying like flies. Florence Nightingale heard about them and wanted to help. She had money to use. So she took 38 nurses and went to the wounded soldiers in the Crimea. The nurses could not believe what they saw. The wounded men had no beds, and no care.

Florence wrote back to the War Department. At first she got no help. But finally the English people heard how bad the situation was, and Florence got help. For the first time in history, wounded men got decent care. The wounded soldiers worshiped Florence.

"At first," Emily wrote, "nobody would listen to her. But now the whole nation is back of her!"

"Maybe," Elizabeth thought, "just maybe, someday, America will be back of women doctors."

Elizabeth had been in New York for four years now. She had no friends except the Quakers. They came to her office and brought other patients. They supported the dispensary. Elizabeth's days were busy enough.

But she missed the friendship of other people. Male doctors would have nothing to do with her.

She never told her family much about those grim days. Once she did write, "I am glad that I, and not another, have to bear this pioneer work. I understand now why this life has never been lived before. I would like a little fun now and then. Life is altogether too sober."

Chapter *9*

"Impossible!"

By 1856, Elizabeth felt much more cheerful. A few doctors had become her friends. Kitty was good company. Elizabeth enjoyed teaching her just as she had been taught long ago. She often thought of her father, who believed that girls were "thinking creatures." One day a doctor friend came to the office to visit with Elizabeth. When he had gone, Kitty said, "Doctor, how very odd to hear a man called 'doctor'!" Elizabeth laughed out loud. How long, she wondered, had it been since she had laughed that way?

That summer Emily came home from Europe, and Marie graduated. Elizabeth took over more of her house to make offices for the three of them. Her Quaker friends brought more patients. Soon all three doctors were busy. Then one night Elizabeth shocked them with an idea. She thought they ought to open an infirmary—a small hospital.

There were two medical colleges for women now. But their graduates had no chance to intern in the best hospitals.

Elizabeth had already found a house. It was big enough to be turned into a small hospital. They could rent it for $1,300 a year.

"Impossible!" Emily said.

Elizabeth smiled. "I think I've heard that before."

Many people agreed with Emily. It was impossible! However, Elizabeth's Quaker friends, some other friends, and well-to-do businessmen thought it was a good idea. They put up the money.

Just a year later, in May of 1857, the New York Infirmary for Women and Children opened. From the beginning, it had special features that no other hospital had. There was an outpatient department, to take care of poor people after they went home.

There was a "sanitary visitor" who went to tenement homes to teach mothers about the importance of sanitation—cleanliness, fresh air, and sunshine.

Dr. Rebecca Cole, the first black woman doctor, was the first sanitary visitor. She did a fine job, and later she trained other doctors in the work.

Careful records were kept in the infirmary of every patient, every intern, and every nurse. Soon doctors came from other hospitals to study those records.

The infirmary was just a year old when Elizabeth announced, "I'm going to England for a while."

Emily gasped. "Why?"

Elizabeth's friends in England were still fighting for a chance to study in a medical college. They kept writing, begging her to help. Maybe she could wake up the British by making speeches.

"They need me more than you do," Elizabeth said. "You and Marie can handle everything here."

Kitty looked worried. "What will I do, my doctor? Will you send me back to the orphanage?"

"Of course not! You'll stay with some of our family until I get back. And never let me hear you say 'orphanage' again!" Then she laughed and hugged Kitty.

Every time Elizabeth spoke to a group in England, people begged her to stay there. If only she would stay, she could get things done.

"Our pioneering in America is not finished," she said. "It has been only ten years since the first woman doctor graduated. Maybe in another ten years women will have a better chance in medicine."

She went to see Florence Nightingale and could hardly hide her shock. A severe illness during the war, and hard work, had wrecked her health. She was an invalid, working mostly from her bed.

After the war a grateful nation had set up a fund of more than $150,000 in Florence's name. Florence was planning to use the money to found a school for training nurses. Please, she begged, wouldn't Elizabeth stay and take charge of the school?

Elizabeth had to say no.

"Sometimes," Elizabeth wrote to Emily, "I spend more time saying no than I do making speeches!"

Then she ended that letter with a very special piece of news. She was the first, and only, woman physician listed in the British Medical Registry. Only ten years had passed since she became Dr. Blackwell. Things did move at a lively pace, didn't they?

Chapter *10*

"What's Done Is Done"

Elizabeth told her friends in England that she intended to found a medical college for women. Doctors trained there could intern in the infirmary. As soon as the college opened, English girls would be welcomed.

In August of 1859 Elizabeth got home. The infirmary had become well known. More and more doctors came to visit it and to ask questions.

Marie had gone to Boston to take charge of a hospital there. Emily was an excellent director. She had trained some fine interns from the women's medical colleges.

Elizabeth began planning for the college she would found. She hoped to open it in three years, by 1862. But in April 1861 the Civil War began. Planning for the college ended. Years of long, hard work began.

Elizabeth called a meeting of the infirmary staff to plan to train nurses for the War Department. Word of the meeting happened to get into a newspaper. A mob of women crowded into the infirmary. Others filled the street outside.

Elizabeth knew she would need more room for volunteers to wait. Peter Cooper, a very rich and generous New Yorker, had built Cooper Union, a school where needy young people could get a free college education.

He let Elizabeth use a big hall at Cooper Union for the interviews. Day after day Elizabeth sat at a desk there and interviewed women who wanted to become nurses.

Bellevue Hospital offered to give the nurses special training for their work with the War Department. Sometimes Elizabeth smiled to herself. Bellevue Hospital would not have accepted her as an intern. But now those same doctors let her choose the nurses to be trained at Bellevue.

At last the war ended, and Elizabeth's job was done. For the last time she walked from Cooper Union back to the infirmary. It seemed to take her forever.

"Dr. Blackwell," a nurse said, "you need a good long rest!"

"What we need," Elizabeth said, "is to get that college started."

There was no rest for Elizabeth until the college opened. It started many new practices. For the first time there were entrance examinations for students. There were three years of training and longer school terms. Every student had to take the course in hygiene—preventive medicine.

Three-fourths of the faculty were men —willing and eager to work with those two Blackwell doctors!

Elizabeth taught the course in hygiene and also handled problems of all kinds. She still had not found time for that "good long rest." She looked paler and more tired each day.

"Elizabeth," Emily pleaded, "you've got to get some rest."

"You're absolutely right. I'm going to give up my work here."

"What?" Emily gasped.

"What's done is done. I will leave it."

Word spread like wildfire through the college and the infirmary.

"You do need a good long rest," a nurse said.

"I'm going back to England," Elizabeth told her.

The nurse smiled. "A nice long sea voyage will fix you up!"

"Yes, it certainly will." Elizabeth turned to Kitty. "We'll have to start packing."

Elizabeth had not known how tired she was until they were on the ship and in their cabin. She lay down.

"Kitty, I'm a wretched sailor. I'll be right here the whole voyage. But there is no need for you to stay with me. I want you to stay on deck and enjoy yourself."

"Aunt Elizabeth, I'm no child. I'm 22. You took care of me when I needed it. Now I'll take care of you."

Elizabeth gave her a long, level stare. Then she said, "Yes, doctor!"

They both laughed.

When they left the ship in Liverpool, Kitty said, "We're going to find a nice, quiet place to rest before we go to London."

"Just for a few days," Elizabeth said.

The rest lasted for a few weeks, but finally Elizabeth began dictating speeches to Kitty.

"People here need to know that 'prevention is better than cure,'" she told Kitty.

After they reached London, Elizabeth was soon as busy as ever. Patients flocked to her office. People begged her to speak. If anybody could get women accepted in English medical schools, Dr. Blackwell was the one to do it!

In spite of everything she could do or say, the English medical colleges still said no to women.

Elizabeth did succeed in something else that was close to her heart. She organized the National Health Society, to teach people how to keep well. A friend made an emblem for the society. On it was Elizabeth's favorite motto: "Prevention is better than cure." The society soon made a name for itself. It also made more demands on Elizabeth's time.

Kitty was a wonderful help. She ran the office. She wrote the speeches and articles that Elizabeth dictated. In spite of all Kitty's help, sometimes it seemed there were not enough hours in the day.

Friends worried about Elizabeth. She looked so pale. She really ought to slow down, they said. Elizabeth's only answer was, "There's still work to do!"

Finally Elizabeth knew what Kitty had known for quite a while. She would have to choose between her practice and her fight for women to have doctor's training in England. She could not do both.

At last the first medical college for women opened in England.

Elizabeth's fight was won. "I'm ready to retire now," she said.

"If the world will let you retire," was Kitty's answer.

Chapter 11

"Your Work Goes On!"

Elizabeth bought a home, Rock House, near Hastings, on the southern coast of England. It overlooked the sea.

She took long walks, felt the sea breeze, and watched the beautiful ships. She did so love ships—from dry land!

Soon everyone nearby knew her—especially the poor people and the horses. She always answered a call from the poor, and she always had carrots for the horses.

People from all over the world came to her door with questions and problems. Kitty took care of letters and visitors.

Every mail from America brought wonderful news. The number of women doctors in America had reached 3,000, then 4,500, then 7,000. Better yet, many of the older medical colleges were admitting women.

Friends begged Elizabeth to write a book about her early struggles.

"Nonsense," she said, "that's all past and forgotten. Nobody would want to read about it now."

Friends still begged. At last she wrote *Pioneer Work in Opening the Medical Profession to Women.* One printing after another sold out. The book brought her letters from all over the world.

Elizabeth and Kitty went back once for a brief visit to America.

An old friend who was a doctor looked at Elizabeth keenly. They understood each other.

She lifted her eyebrows. "So I won't live to be a hundred."

"No," he said, "you'll die one of these days. But the pioneer work you did will grow until it covers the world! What courage it must have taken!"

"Mostly stubbornness," she said. "I was always a very stubborn woman."

Family and friends were there to wave good-bye when her ship sailed. Many of them were crying.

But Elizabeth smiled at Kitty. "One nice thing about it. I'll never have to make this trip again!"

And she did not. She died at Rock House in the spring of 1910. She was a stubborn pioneer whose work goes on and on. .